What bald men are sa'

MW00769557

"Dave Beswick's 101 ways to use your head and win with skin is unparalleled in the history of baldomidity. If you're bald, ever speak in front of people and are willing to poke a little fun at yourself, this book gives you all the bald one-liners you'll ever need."
— Dick Vitale, ESPN Sports

"This is such an important book!"
— Jon Miller, ESPN baseball commentator

"The 9 ways to experience nature head-on has given me a new appreciation for my balding head as a wonderful receptor for the sun, wind, rain, and occasional tree. This is a book to be *used*, not just read."
— Frank Marrero, author of
Lincoln Beachey, The Man Who Owned the Sky

"Whenever I use my head as a bowling ball or have kids lay their hands on my head to make a special wish, people around me get happier. If you're ready to smile, chuckle and laugh, read this book."
— Tim Payne, principal of
Fort Dorchester High School,
North Charleston, S.C.

"Did you know that bald men are the first ones to hear snowflakes and never have to re-fix their hair after being caught in the rain? These and 14 other 'fringe benefits' await the fortunate reader of this delightful book."
— Allen King, Senior Vice-President
of Bank First in Tennessee

What others are saying about this book:

"This book is humorous. It'd be a good gift for someone whose upper-level real estate has expanded. But in addition to being light-hearted it sends a positive message."
— Sam Venable, *Knoxville News Sentinel*

"Dave Beswick offers humor and hope for the bald and the beautiful."
— Mark Curnutte, *The Cincinnati Enquirer*

"The author is urging his fellow baby boomers to embrace hair-free heads with the same passion they threw into growing hair in their 20s and 30s. He plans to reverse the several-thousand-year-old superstition that people with hair are sexier, stronger, and smarter than the bald."
— Betty Booker, *Richmond Times Dispatch*

"A humorous and highly entertaining book. A quick read that will bring a smile to anyone's face."
— Jim Melfi, *The St. Augustine Chronicle*

"Dave Beswick is at peace with his baldness. He's so comfortable with his 'cranial nudity' that he's written a book to help others cope with the often taboo topic of hair loss."
— Kevin Donlin, *The Citizens' Voice*
Wilkes-Barre, Pennsylvania

"*Bald Men Always Come Out on Top* is a winner. Dave Beswick has inspired a powerful program of appreciation by turning a loss into a real gain through anecdotes. He has turned an affliction into a new way of life."
— Bill Finley, *Senior Life and Boomer Times*
Boca Raton, Florida

Bald Men Always Come Out on Top

101 Ways to Use Your Head
and
Win with Skin

Dave Beswick

Ama Publishing

St. Augustine, Florida

Bald Men Always Come Out on Top

101 Ways to Use Your Head
and
Win with Skin

by Dave Beswick

Published by: **Ama Publishing**
Post Office Box 840117
St. Augustine Beach, FL. 32084-0117 U.S.A.

Printed in the United States of America

Illustrations by Diane English

ISBN 0-9613176-1-2

LCCN 95-95139

A Note To the Reader

At the present time, there are approximately 432 million bald men in the world. Two-thirds of all men are bald or balding by age 65 and $2 billion a year is spent, in the United States alone, on hair growth and hair replacement products.

When losing our hair, we have five options. We can:

1. Wear a hat most of the time or comb long strands over our bald spots

2. Get a toupee or be specially fitted for a hair weave

3. Apply a hair-growth medication to the crown of our heads

4. Have surgical scalp reductions, hair lifts, and micrograftings done

5. Learn to accept what we've been given and make the most of it

In other words, we can choose to make new waves or let the tide roll out to sea. We can put on a new roof or leave the dome alone.

If we think that baldness is a problem that needs to be solved, we will likely choose one or more of the first four options. If we believe that hair is essential to being sexually attractive, getting a good job, or to feeling more confident and secure, we will likely choose among options two, three, and four. On the other hand, if we have come to accept that we are likable and attractive with *or* without hair then it doesn't matter what we decide to do with our heads. *Bald Men Always Come Out on Top* is the guidebook for those who have chosen or are considering option five.

This book is specially dedicated to an enormous sub-culture of wonderful men who are happily hairless. These lustrous wonders have been making people smile and laugh for decades by faithfully repeating the traditional bald favorites that have been handed down to them for generations. "Grass doesn't grow on a busy street," "A rolling stone gathers no moss," and "There's only one sure way to save your hair: in a cigar box" were part of a mere handful of expressions they parroted from the bald oral tradition. By substantially adding to the limited collection of bald humor, this book of humorful wisdom pays special tribute to these millions of hairfree men who bring joy into our lives.

About the Author

Dave Beswick was fourteen when he first started losing his hair. At least twice a day he would go into the bathroom, lock the door, and gaze anxiously at his reflection in the mirror. He was deathly afraid of losing his hair because, like many men with recessive genes, he had unknowingly inherited the following eight negative beliefs about baldness:

1. Baldness is a problem that needs to be solved.

2. I can solve the problem by doing one or more of the following: wear a hat, comb my hair over the bald areas, get a hair addition like a toupee or weave, have hair replacement surgery, or use a hair growth medication.

3. Women are not attracted to bald(ing) men.

4. I need hair to be sexually attractive.

5. I need hair to look and feel younger.

6. It's okay for older men to be bald, but not younger ones like me.

7. I need hair to feel secure, confident, and socially at ease.

8. Having hair is key to finding a good job and being successful.

Like most men, Dave was a problem-solver. He was used to identifying problems and finding solutions for them. Since he had improved his appearance and feeling of well-being by changing his diet and exercising regularly, he unconsciously assumed that he could personally do something to alter his hair loss as well.

In searching for a solution to his "problem," he went to a dermatologist, a hair restoration clinic, and for years stood on his head and massaged his scalp daily to get the blood flowing to the follicles. He also tried lotions, vibrators, tonics, and creams—all to no avail. In the meantime, he did the best he could by fluffing up the hair he had and spreading it over the balding areas.

Feeling frustrated and angry that his locks were heading south out of his control, he gradually got the message that his hair loss could not be changed by any willful effort on his part. He saw the handwriting on the head of his familial predecessors and knew that if new hair was ever to appear on his head again, it would have to come from some outside intervention. Toupees, rudimentary hair weaves, and the first phase of hair transplantation were the options available to him. After carefully weighing the pros and cons of each option, he chose to live with his growing face and make the best of it.

He stopped wearing his baseball hat as a cover-up and began redirecting his attention from the top of his peak to what was going on *inside* his head. He learned an important lesson that would impact the rest of his life: he did not choose to be bald, but he could choose how he thought about it and how he responded to it.

He discovered for himself that all the negative beliefs about baldness that he had been given were false, and that believing in them only made him feel worse about his cranial expansion. Thus, he identified the specific negative beliefs that had been in his mind for decades and changed them into positive beliefs that exist to this day. Having changed his mind about his parting of the waves, Dave finally recognized that he was attractive to many women and knew that who he was was far more important than how much hair he had on his pate.

He began having fun with his head around friends, children, strangers, and work associates and found that he could actually flaunt what he didn't have and elicit smiles and laughter wherever he went. He began asking for estimates at barber shops, letting toddlers use his head as a superhighway for their toy cars, and telling people that he was the president of *The Skin Club for Men*. He eventually wrote down all that came to him about the bald head over a twenty-five period which issued forth into this largest collection of positive bald humor in the world.

Acknowledgments

To my wife and best friend, Janie, I am deeply appreciative for your constant love and support and for your wonderful suggestions in the writing of this book. You have been there every step of the way and have patiently responded whenever I needed your help. You are a beautiful person inside and out and I am blessed by the tremendous joy, love, and laughter you bring into my life.

And thank you, Diane English, for your whimsical illustrations. Without you, this book would be just words; with you, the book comes alive. Dan Poynter, I am most grateful for your instruction, resources, and ongoing help in the production and promotion of this book. And to you Janet Lydecker, thanks very much for your *sterling* suggestions and loving support.

Cover design by Izen Player and Robert Howard
Cover layout and design work by Regine de Toledo of Graphics Ink
Editing by Stacey Lynn
Book design and typography by Chris Nolt of Cirrus Design
Book printed by Patterson Printing

Contents

The author at birth

The author today

Introduction

This book is specially written for you sensuous, sensitive, loving, fun, and intelligent men who are happily hairless. It is for those of you who have come to peace with your head and are ready to use your beautiful bean as a positive asset for your own and others' enjoyment.

What do most women really want in a man? Is hair near the top of the list? The first chapter goes beneath the skin to find these revealing answers.

Have you ever been hair-assed by a hair lover or insensitive mane-iac and wished you had something clever to say in return? This book gives you 42 witty responses whenever your sculptured speed bump becomes the focus of attention. For example, retorts such as, "Remember, my friend, the nearer the bone, the sweeter the meat," or "My bald head is a solar-energy panel for a sex machine," will inevitably leave you with the last word.

In "The Fringe Benefits and the Hairiness of Being Bald," you now have 32 unique things to say about the perks and disadvantages of cranial nudity. One such benefit is that you can be spotted easily by loved ones in a crowd. Another advantage is that you never have to worry which way you're facing in the wind. On the other hand, you cannot easily hide in a crowd and it takes longer to dry your face when using those electric wall dryers.

If you like the outdoors, you will soon learn 9 glorious ways to experience nature head-on in a way that people with hair cannot. If you dare to bare in the open air, and let the sun, wind, rain, and fog caress your crest, you're in for some purely pate enjoyment.

Another fun way to use your head is to invite people to answer *Bald Trivia* questions. Find out who the bald expert is in your group by seeing who gets the most right out of the 38 possibilities.

In order to truly understand and appreciate your place in history, it is important to acknowledge the renowned bald men past and present who have left their mark on the world. In "Famous Bald Men: A Distinguished Hairitage," you have a list of 108 bald men who have successfully used their heads and come out on top. Sensing their accomplishments and the impact they have made on millions of people can serve to strengthen your identity as a baldheaded man and enhance your appreciation for what your clean slate has to offer.

In "Debunking the Myths about Hair Loss," you will learn how to distinguish between old wives' tales, outright fallacies, and the truth about hair loss. Does shampooing daily, wearing hats, brushing your hair one hundred times a day, or having too much sex cause baldness? Is it hereditary? Does lying on a slant board, shaving your head, or massaging your scalp daily help to grow it back? After reading this chapter, you'll be able to respond intelligently and humorously to these most frequently asked questions about hair loss.

Are you the type of man who would prefer doing something rather than just talking about it? You now have at your fingertips 32 practical ways to have fun with your head and bring humor to bare in a variety of situations. For instance, carry a comb and pull it out once in a while and say, "Would you like a comb? Up 'til now I haven't been able to part with it." Or, while standing in line at a checkout counter, moan to the person in front of you, "Whew, I'm having a bad hair day!"

In the chapters entitled, "The Bald Head: A Spiritual Symbol" and "Ode to Hair," you have poetic renderings relating some of the universal verities that can be gleaned from reflecting on the bald head. And finally, in "Bald Mind: Wis-dome for the Bald Soul," you are invited to ponder the admonitions for living with greater insight, humor, and love on the bald path.

Enjoy this book, and above all, have fun with your head. Now that you've stopped making waves, a whole new world of cranial comedy awaits your personal rendition. Use what works for you and you'll definitely experience that marvelous feeling of what it means to win with skin.

Spread the news that bald men are . . .

Millions of Women Declare: "We Want More Than Hair!"

Right now, the bald truth is that millions of women on this planet are attracted to and love maneless men.

Discerning women know that fine feathers do not necessarily make fine birds—that hair does *not* make the man. They scoff at cover-ups of any sort and call for the real thing. Granted, there are some women who prefer men with hair, just as there are those who would clearly opt for a bald man when given the choice. It is important to realize that just because women can appreciate men with hair does not mean that they are *only* attracted to those with locks.

For most women, the way a man looks is important, but not nearly as important as who he is, what he is willing to live and die for, and how loving and secure he is within himself. It's not hair they want, but rather men with core spiritual values who are able to love and care for themselves, others, and the planet. They are looking for responsible men who are not only good persons, but also good husbands and providers. For those choosing to have children, being a loving father is paramount in their list of values.

Hair, body physique, and other externals are always secondary to these discriminating women who know that what lies beneath the surface is far more important than how much hair a man may possess. Whereas the majority of men tend to judge women by their physical appearance, most women do not follow the same standards. Rather, they tend to look at men on the *whole* and are far more accepting of their idiosyncrasies than men tend to be of women.

These women of substance want more than a man in sheep's clothing. They want a man who listens to and respects their needs and desires without pushing them off to the side. They want a man who allows himself to feel and who can express his feelings in a direct and nonreactive way.

A positive bald man who builds a full head of self-esteem by consistently following his heart's desire is naturally appealing. He is comfortable with his head and thus others are easeful with it too. By moving from the inside out and standing firm as the winds of status quo attempt to steer him off his course, he commands respect as a man of integrity and commitment.

A bald man with a spontaneous and uplifting sense of humor brings delight and joy to the already sumptuous table of relationship. Such humor tells the woman that he somehow understands; that he knows that life is short and that there is not a lot of time to waste by taking things, like hair loss, too seriously. Humor lightens the load, opens the heart and body, and releases endorphins everywhere.

Thus, a wise women does not judge a man by his cover, but by the amount of love he has in his heart. In the end, the quality with which he is able to love will stand forth as the most cherished attribute of all.

"What He hath scanted men in hair,
He hath given them in wit."
—*William Shakespeare*

Forty-Two Witty Ways to Respond Whenever You Are Being Hair-assed or Your Bald Head Becomes the Focus of Attention

If you are willing to poke fun at yourself and to have fun with your head, people will laugh *with* you. Think about it—don't you always laugh when someone jokes about a particular part of his or her anatomy? Good comedians get a lot of mileage out of this age-old form of humor by bringing the obvious right out in the open—and so can you! As an added benefit, every time you flaunt your threadbare epidermis for the sake of others' enjoyment, you will enhance your self-esteem *and* deepen your appreciation for that classy chassis known as your head.

Ways to respond whenever your bald head becomes the focus of attention

- I used to have waves—
  now all I have is the beach.

- Bald men always outgrow their hair.

- They only put marble on top
  of the finest furniture.

- Bald business owners have little overhead.

- Hairful man say: Man who has no hair
  has no part. Hairful man wrong.

- In an educated English accent say,
  "I'm not combing impaired, good sir,
  but intelligence affluent."

- In a similar accent say,
  "Nor am I follicly challenged,
  but rather free from greasy fleece."

- Last year a bald man won the National
  Blow-Drying Championship, by more than a hair.

- I have been headily aerodynamic for years
  now and my wife loves it. She's always been
  fond of melons.

- Bald Sage says:
  Bald man who wears toupee on hill,
  Not on level.

- Bald surgeons are smooth operators.

- When someone asks why or how you lost your hair, answer, "The Lord giveth and the Lord taketh away."

- I have wavy hair—one hair waves to the other.

- Bald men are most levelheaded. No one ever gets in their hair.

- I went into the marines and got a crew cut. The only trouble is, my crew bailed out early.

- Bald men are among the few, the proud, and the bald.

- Hair Trigger:
  1. A propensity toward premature ejaculation.
  2. What Roy Rogers used to say when calling his horse.

- Thin is in. Who wants fat hair anyway?

- Morehead City, North Carolina—good place for a bald baby to be born.
  Seymore Head—good name for a bald baby.

- "It's nothing to pull your hair out over." (To be said as an icebreaker in a tense situation.)

- Bald men are ahead of their time.

Bald Men Are Ahead of Their Time

"Harry!"

Ways to respond whenever you are being hair-assed

Hair-assment: the persistent teasing of a bald man by someone having a hair affair.

- We're all born with the same number of hormones; if you want to use yours for growing hair, that's your business!

- The nearer the bone, the sweeter the meat.

- My hair's not getting longer, it's just sliding off the back of my head.

- Real men don't use combs.

- Your libido (sexual drive) does not live in your hair.

- I just took the "Test Your Own Testosterone Challenge" and came out on top for the third year in a row.

- Off the top of my head, I have nothing to say.

- Yes, split hair is a problem. Mine split about five years ago.

- "FOLLIC OFF, FURBALL!" — to be said only to those hairful fellows who deliberately usurp the crown.

- Baldness, like classic beauty, is only skin deep.

The weekly meeting of
H̲air A̲ddicts A̲nonymous

- I'm not going bald, I'm just starting a second face.

- All people are bald up to their hairline.

- Being bald is a great way to be. I mean, let's face it, who else is slippery like an eel, as smooth as glass, and clean as a whistle all at the same time?

- How long have you been addicted to hair?

- Don't judge a book by its cover,
  nor a bald man by his nubber.

- My bald head is a solar-energy panel
  for a sex machine.

- I may lack luster,
  but the ladies still cluster.

It is important to respond humorously when others make quips about our pearly pates. However, this approach has not always been followed, as the prophet Elisha reports:

> From Jericho he went to Bethel.
> As he was walking along the road
> some young boys from the city
> began mocking and making fun of
> him because of his bald head. He
> turned around and cursed them in
> the name of the Lord; and two
> female bears came out of the woods
> and killed forty-two of them.
> Kings 2: 23-25

Oldies But Goodies: Traditional Bald Favorites

- The Lord is just; the Lord is fair.
  He gave some brains, and others hair.

- There's only one sure way to save
  your hair—in a cigar box.

- Grass doesn't grow on a busy street.

- A rolling stone gathers no moss.

- God created a few perfect heads;
  the rest he covered with hair.

- There's only one thing that stops
  falling hair—the floor.

- If you're bald on top,
  you're a great thinker.

  If you're bald in back,
  you're a great lover.

  If you're bald all over,
  you think you're a great lover.

(3)

The Fringe Benefits and the Hairiness of Being Bald

In order to truly accept your head as it is, it is essential to embrace both the benefits and the disadvantages (the hairiness) of being bald. With this chapter, you now have 32 particular things to say about the perks and drawbacks of having a lean bean. For maximum impact, stress the benefits.

Since every benefit has a corresponding disadvantage, you might find it helpful to read the following columns from left to right. For example, a benefit of being bald is that you spend little money on hair care products, while the corresponding disadvantage is that you can end up spending more money on hats and other head coverings.

Fringe Benefits	The Hairiness of Being Bald
You can be spotted easily by loved ones in a crowd (e.g., in a movie theater).	You cannot hide easily in a crowd.

Fringe Benefits

It provides more open space for your partner to kiss and caress.

You are the first one to hear snowflakes and you have built-in air conditioning.

It feels great when your dog, as a member of the clean pate club, licks your head till it shines.

You get sun kissed and feel a soothing warmth penetrating your scalp.

You never have to worry which way you're facing in the wind.

You don't get dandruff (you're not a flake) and never have a bad hair day.

The Hairiness of Being Bald

It can be embarrassing when you forget to wipe the lipstick off your head.

Your head gets cold more easily, and you can lose up to 75 percent of your body heat through the top of your head.

Bugs use your head as a landing strip.

You get sunburned.

It takes longer to dry your face when using those electric wall dryers.

You perspire on top after eating spicy foods.

Baldness has its perks . . .

You're easier to find in a dark theater

Fringe Benefits

You don't have to dry, re-shampoo, or re-fix your hair after being caught in the rain.

Hairballs no longer collect in the corners of your bathroom.

It makes a one-step out of brain surgery.

You have less to be self-involved about.

You're always clearheaded and never split hairs with anyone.

The Hairiness of Being Bald

Rain rolls more easily into your eyes and onto your clothes, like water off a duck's back.

It takes longer to wash your face.

It hurts when you hit your peak on low chandeliers, low entryways, and open cabinet doors.

You have more to be vain about (i.e., your virile appearance).

You get called names like "slicko," "shiner," "skinhead," "air head," "cue ball," and "curly."

Shriner

Shiner

Fringe Benefits	The Hairiness of Being Bald
You stay looking the same age for a long period of time.	You can get sunspots, white spots, and even cancer spots if you expose yourself too much.
You can swim faster and don't have to wear swim caps.	The chlorine and salt water can dry out, starch, and stretch your delicate head skin.
You spend very little money on haircuts and hair care products.	You spend more money on hats and other head coverings.
It's very time efficient (e.g., you can be ready faster than anyone in the morning or after working out).	You spend too much of your extra time watching sports on TV, hanging out on the couch, and shaping your "love handles."

For more benefits of being bald, turn to the next chapter and discover how you can enjoy nature in a way that people with hair can only dream about.

Nine Ways to Experience Nature Head-On in a Way That People with Hair Cannot

For millions of us hair free men, being unencumbered with forestation on our northern parcel produces unparalleled titillating feelings. Women running their fingers across our skin is pure excitement. Feeling the softness of our pet's fur up against our craniums is tenderness at its best, while being openended in the fog is nothing short of exhilarating. And when you stop and think about it, only us domers can get a brain massage simply by standing under a shower head.

If you like the outdoors, you're heartily invited to try any of these nine glorious ways to experience nature head-on in a way that people with hair cannot. If you dare to bare in the open air, and let the sun, wind, rain, and fog caress your crest, you're in for some purely pate enjoyment.

Sun Kissing*

1. Sit outside in a comfortable chair for about 10 minutes and feel the warmth of the sun on your head. Visualize and feel the sun's golden-white light moving down from your head throughout your whole body. Feel the warm rays sending healing heat and positive energy to all your organs, especially to those areas that are cramped or need some loosening up.

Breeze Brushing

2. As you sit or walk outside, feel the air brushing over your head. Feel its refreshing coolness invigorating your body, or its soothing warmth helping to quiet and calm. Let the aroma of nature into your lungs and enjoy whatever poetry the breezes bring.

Water Wallowing

3. As you stand in the shower, let the warm water massage your scalp and relish the warmth penetrating your body.

* These exercises are FOR BALD MEN ONLY. Please discourage your hairy friends from trying these activities as they will only become disheartened at not being able to fully partake in these baldiferous pleasures.

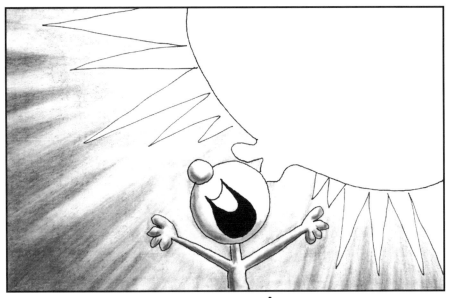

Sun Kissed

4. When it rains, go outside and delight in the droplets bouncing off your head. Hear the sound of the falling rain and feel the stimulation this heavenly shower brings. Then, stick out your tongue and taste the raindrops falling into your mouth.

5. Never pass up the refreshing opportunity to stand directly under a natural or human-made waterfall on a hot summer day. Let your eyes behold and body feel the penetrating coolness of the water. Let yourself laugh as your naked noggin goes head to head with one of nature's mellifluous wonders. Be careful of tiny pebbles or debris that may drop down from the natural falls.

6. Submerge in a Jacuzzi and luxuriate in this most nurturing feeling. Imagine you are back in the womb and floating in the warm fluid. Then, place the top of your head close to one of the jets for a brain-stimulating thrill.

Fog Misting

7. Being in the buff in the fog is a rare treat because it's the one time clouds actually come to you. Let the cool fog gently moisturize your head while you take in slow, invigorating breaths.

Nature Sensing

8. Rub your head gently underneath a smooth green leaf or your favorite plant or flower. Feel the energy coming from the plant through the top of your head. And while sunbathing, put suntan lotion on top of your head and use your head to massage it all over your loved one's body. A nurturing, tender, and sensuous experience.

Pet Caressing

9. Luxuriate in one of the warmest feelings available to us. Simply move your head up against your pet and feel the softness and warmth of your dear friend's fur and skin.

Hair today, gone tomorrow
Do not lament nor feel such sorrow.
For all that comes surely goes,
From the top of the head
To the end of the toes.

(5)

Bald Trivia

Another fun way to use your head is to invite people to answer bald trivia questions. Find out who the bald expert is in your group and offer a prize to the one who gets the most right.

1. What is the one sure thing that stops falling hair?
   — The floor

2. Name three bald movie actors.
   — Yul Brenner, Sean Connery, Telly Savalas, Danny Devito, Lou Gosset, Jr., Sir John Gielgud

3. What did the bailiff say when announcing the entrance of the bald judge?
   — "Hair ye, hair ye, please rise."

4. Positive bald men are sensuous, loving, fun, and intelligent. True or false?
   — True

5. What mountain do bald men like to climb?
   — Bald Mountain or Mt. Baldy

6. Who is the most handsome bald man you know?
   — You (the only correct answer)

7. Name a bald movie producer.
   — Carl Reiner, Rob Reiner, Ron Howard, Cecil B. De Mille

8. How did the bald man strain his neck?
   — King Kong used him as a roll-on

9. Two former prime ministers of Israel were bald. Can you name one of them?
   — Menachem Begin, Yitzhak Rabin

10. Bald monks are aerodynamically designed to go straight to heaven. True or false?
    — True

11. Name three famous naturally bald athletes (not ones who shaved their heads) from three different sports.
      — Y. A. Tittle, Terry Bradshaw (football)
        Kareem Abdul-Jabbar (basketball)
        Sam Snead (golf)
        Yogi Berra, Reggie Jackson, Johnny Bench, Gene Tenace, Matt Williams (baseball)
        George Foreman (boxing)

12. What is the bald man's favorite bird?
      — The bald eagle

13. Who is the famous bald African-American agricultural scientist who developed 300 uses for the peanut?
      — George Washington Carver

14. Too much sex causes baldness. True or false?
      — False

15. Name 3 U.S. Presidents who were bald.
      — George Washington, John Adams, John Quincy Adams, Martin Van Buren, James Garfield, Dwight D. Eisenhower, and Gerald Ford

16. Name three advantages of being bald.
    — Anything people come up with is correct.

    Here are some of the fringe benefits. See chapter 3 for the full list.

    • You can be spotted easily in a crowd.
    • There's more space to be kissed and caressed.
    • You don't get dandruff.
    • You don't have to worry which way you're facing in the wind.
    • It makes a one-step out of brain surgery.

17. Name a former president of Egypt who was happily hairless.
    — Anwar Sadat

18. What did the bald man leave in his will?
    — A hairloom

19. What is the name of a very well-known bald prime minister of Great Britain?
    — Sir Winston Churchill

20. Name one bald sports commentator.
    — Dick Vitale, basketball commentator
        for ESPN Sports
      Joe Garagiola, TV baseball commentator
      Jon Miller, TV baseball commentator for
        ESPN and radio broadcaster for the
        Baltimore Orioles

21. Name the bald British naturalist, famous for his
    theories of evolution.
    — Charles Darwin

22. What do the letters B - A - L - D stand for?
    (Invite people to take their time in thinking about
    this answer, and be ready for some off-the-wall
    responses.) Any answer shedding a positive light
    on the bald head is correct. Here are some
    answers to mention after all the responses
    come in:
    a. Bald And Lacking Dandruff
    b. Bad Ass Lean Dude
    c. Bald men Are Loved Dearly

23. Name the former bald President of France.
    — Charles De Gaulle

24. What is the name of the famous bald Spanish artist who was a dominant figure in the art of the 1900s?
— Pablo Picasso

25. What is the bald man's favorite tree?
— The bald cypress tree

26. Name two Soviet leaders who were bald.
— Vladimir Lenin, Nikita Krushchev, and Mikhail Gorbachev

27. What is the psychological term used to describe a bald man who blames someone or something else for his hair loss?
— Overhead projection

28. Name one Catholic pope who was bald.
— Pope John XXIII
Pope Paul VI

29. What bald American author wrote *The Seven Habits of Highly Effective People*?
— Stephen R. Covey

30. What is the bald man's favorite spot?
Any of the following answers are correct
(it depends on the individual's preference):
a. Hot spot
b. Soft spot
c. Bald spot
d. G spot
e. Wet spot
f. Hawaii

31. Who was the famous bald Hindu saint and
nationalist of India?
— Mahatma Gandhi

32. What was the first bourgeois cure for baldness
created by a Frenchman?
— The guillotine

33. Name the bald English playwright considered
to be the greatest dramatist the world has
ever known.
— William Shakespeare

34. Even Harry can be bald. True or false?
— True

35. Name a bald prime minister of Canada.
    — Pierre Trudeau

36. What do you call a balding adolescent?
    — Oval-teen

37. Who was the former bald premier of China?
    — Chairman Mao Tse-Tung

38. What are the three stages of recession?

— Hairdo		Parted
Hairdid	or	Unparted
Hairdone		Departed

Famous Bald Men: A Distinguished Hairitage

Simply by letting nature take its course and trusting that our heads know perfectly well what they need to do, we are granted free membership into a unique and outstanding group of men. The Skin Club for Men? Domers International? Not exactly. By reason of our beaming bulbs alone, we are automatically connected with the remarkable hairitage of bald men past and present.

In order to truly understand and appreciate our place in history, it is important to acknowledge all the great bald men who have come before us as well as those who presently shine in our midst.

Here is a list of 108 bald men who have successfully used their heads and come out on top. Whether they be famous entertainers, musicians, writers, world leaders, politicians, sport figures, or spiritual giants, they are all passionate men who have made their mark on the world.

As you read these names, allow yourself to become even more empowered as you sense their accomplishments and the impact they have had on the people around them. If an individual brings inspiration, you might listen to what could nourish and actualize that impulse in your own life.

The historical precedent for successful, intelligent, athletic, spiritual, humorous, and powerful bald men is firmly carved in stone. May this lustrous lineage genuinely serve to strengthen your identity and deepen your appreciation for the beautiful bald man that you are.

Actors, Entertainers, Producers

Yul Brenner	*Actor, famous for his role in* The King and I
Sean Connery	*Actor*
Curly (of the 3 Stooges)	*Comic actor*
Jimmy Durante	*Comedian, actor*
Telly Savalas	*Actor*
Danny Devito	*Actor*
Samuel Goldwyn	*Movie mogul*
Ed Asner	*Actor*
Carl Reiner	*Movie actor and producer*
Jason Alexander	*TV actor on "Seinfeld" Show*

Gavin McCloud	*TV actor of "Love Boat" fame*
Phil Silvers	*TV actor*
Dennis Franz	*Head detective on TV's "NYPD Blues"*
Ron Howard	*Actor, movie director, and producer*
Rob Reiner	*Movie actor and director*
Patrick Stuart	*TV actor on series "Star Trek"*
Mark McEwen	*CBS weatherman, cohost of "CBS Morning News"*
Cecil B. De Mille	*Movie producer and director*
Lou Gossett, Jr.	*Actor*
Dave Garraway	*TV commentator for NBC*
Ed Harris	*Actor*
Paul Shaffer	*Band leader on "Dave Letterman Show"*
Sir John Gielgud	*Actor*
Montel Williams	*Talk show host, actor*
Al Roker	*TV interviewer*
Willard Scott	*NBC weatherman on "The Today Show"*

World Leaders

Sir Wilfrid Laurier	*Prime Minister of Canada*
Pierre Trudeau	*Prime Minister of Canada*
Yitzhak Rabin	*Prime Minister of Israel*
Menachem Begin	*Prime Minister of Israel*
Anwar Sadat	*President of Egypt*
Winston Churchill	*Prime Minister of Great Britain*
Vladimir Lenin	*Founder of Soviet Union*
Nikita Krushchev	*Russian leader*
Mikhail Gorbachev	*Russian leader*
Chairman Mao Tse-Tung	*Premier of China*
Charles De Gaulle	*President of France*
Jose Lopez Portillo	*President of Mexico*
Kublai Khan	*Founder of the Mongol dynasty*
Jawaharlal Nehru	*Prime Minister of India*
Peter Stuyvesant	*Director-General of New Netherlands*
Paul von Hindenburg	*President of Germany*
John Jay	*1st Chief Justice of the U.S.*

George Washington	*1st President of the U.S.*
John Adams	*2nd President of the U.S.*
John Quincy Adams	*6th President of the U.S.*
Martin Van Buren	*8th President of the U.S.*
James Garfield	*20th President of the U.S.*
Dwight D. Eisenhower	*34th President of the U.S.*
Gerald Ford	*38th President of the U.S.*

Writers, Artists, Musicians

Time himself is bald
and therefore to the world's end
will have bald followers.
            —William Shakespeare

Eubie Blake	*African-American pianist*
Sigmund Freud	*Austrian physician, father of psychology*
E. E. Cummings	*American poet*
William Shakespeare	*English playwright and poet, considered the greatest dramatist the world has ever known*
Schopenhauer	*German philosopher*
Saint-Saens	*French composer, pianist, organist*

Jean Piaget	*Author, child psychologist*
Alexander Solzhenitsyn	*Exiled Soviet novelist and historian*
George Bernard Shaw	*Irish-born English dramatist, critic, essayist*
Sir William Osler	*Canadian physician and great medical educator*
Fyodor Dostoevsky	*One of greatest writers of Russian literature*
Pablo Picasso	*Spanish artist, dominant figure in the art of the 1900s*
Jacques Offenbach	*German-born French composer of operettas*
Horace Greeley	*Founded New York Tribune newspaper*
Rudyard Kipling	*Leading English author*
Ralph Ellison	*African-American author,* Invisible Man
H. G. Wells	*English novelist, historian*
Stephen R. Covey	*Author renowned for his principle-centered approach to solving personal and professional problems*

Oswald Spengler	*German philosopher, author of* Decline of the West
Wayne Dyer	*Author of books on psychological and spiritual growth*
Thomas Hardy	*English novelist and poet*
Buckminster Fuller	*Renowned American thinker and inventor who designed the geodesic dome*
Sir Noel Coward	*English playwright*
Paul Cezanne	*French artist*
Anton Bruckner	*Austrian composer*
Pablo Casals	*Spanish cellist, one of the greatest musicians of his time*
Charles Darwin	*British naturalist, famous for evolution theories*
Andrei Sakharov	*Soviet Nobel Peace Prize winner for research on thermonuclear reactions*

Social/Political Figures

Linus Pauling	*American chemist, twice awarded Nobel Peace Prize*
George Washington Carver	*African-American agricultural scientist who developed 300 uses for the peanut*
Christopher Columbus	*Italian navigator who opened the New World to exploration*
Georges Clemenceau	*French statesman*
William Jennings Bryan	*American statesman, three times presidential candidate*
Adlai Stevenson	*Democratic nominee for U.S. presidency in 1952 and 1956*
Frank Iacobucci	*Canadian supreme court judge*
John H. Glenn, Jr.	*American astronaut, first to orbit the earth in space, politician*
George Meany	*U.S. labor leader, 1st president of AFL-CIO*
W.E.B. Du Bois	*African-American leader who helped found the N.A.A.C.P.*

William T. Sherman	*Leading Union general in the American Civil War*
Pop Gordy, Jr.	*Gave voice to the African-American experience*
George McGovern	*U.S. representative and senator, Democratic candidate for president in 1972*
Joseph J. Thomson	*Discovered the electron in 1897*
Sam Houston	*Played leading role in Texas' fight for independence from Mexico*
Anthony Comstock	*American social reformer and crusader against vice*

Spiritual Figures

Pope John XXIII	*Beloved pope who initiated the Second Vatican Council*
Swami Vivekananda	*Spiritual teacher of the Hindu tradition*
Thomas Merton	*Catholic monk, writer*
Swami Nityananda	*Spiritual teacher of the Hindu tradition*
Pope Paul VI	*Catholic pope*

St. Ignatius of Loyola	*Founder of the Jesuit order*
Mahatma Gandhi	*Hindu nationalist and saint*
St. Francis of Assisi	*Italian monk, founder of the Franciscan order*
Buddha	*Title of Gautama Siddhartha, Indian philosopher, founder of Buddhism*

Sports Figures

Y. A. Tittle	*NFL quarterback*
Joe Garagiola	*Baseball announcer, TV commentator*
Kareem Abdul-Jabbar	*Basketball legend, the leading scorer in NBA history*
Marvin Hagler	*Professional boxer*
Sam Snead	*Slammin' Sammy won 84 PGA-sanctioned tournaments*
Jon Miller	*Radio and TV baseball commentator*
Tom Landry	*Football coach of the Dallas Cowboys*
Yogi Berra	*NY Yankee baseball great*

Dick Vitale	*ESPN basketball commentator*
George Foreman	*Professional boxer*
Terry Bradshaw	*NFL quarterback and TV commentator*
Gene Tenace	*World Series MVP with Oakland A's*
Michael Jordan	*One of the greatest basketball players of all time*
Reggie Jackson	*Hall of Fame baseball player*
Johnny Bench	*Hall of Fame baseball player with Cincinnati Reds*
Jerry Tarkanian	*College basketball coach with one of the best winning records in college basketball history*

As a sign of solidarity with bald men everywhere, consider joining the "Bald-Headed Men of America" Club. Founded by John T. Capps III, its motto is, "If you haven't got it, flaunt it!" John also points out, "It's a case of mind over matter. If you don't mind, it doesn't matter."

For a $10 contribution you are sent a certificate, a membership card with your name and number on it, and a *Bald Is Beautiful* poem. And periodically you will receive a copy of their newsletter *Chrome Dome*. An annual B.M.A. convention is held in Morehead City, N. Carolina. For membership information, write to

Bald-Headed Men of America
102 Bald Dr.
Morehead City, N.C. 28557
Include a stamped, self-addressed envelope.

Debunking the Myths about Hair Loss

The purpose of this chapter is to help you distinguish between old wives' tales, half-truths, outright fallacies, and the truth about hair loss. After reading this chapter, you'll be able to respond intelligently and humorously to these most frequently asked questions about baldness:

Does shampooing twice a day, thinking too much, wearing hats, brushing your hair one hundred times a day, or having sex too often cause baldness? Is it hereditary? Does lying on a slant board, hanging upside down regularly on a back swing, shaving your head, or massaging your scalp daily help to grow hair back or at least save the hair you have? Is there a cure on the horizon?

Most of the following information will also be useful to you when dealing with younger men who are having a hard time accepting their follicular atrophy. Since they frequently try many of these hair saving

Male Pattern Baldness

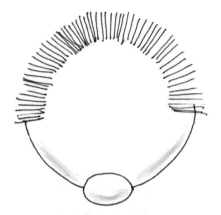

The Monk Fringe

The 5 Strand Flip

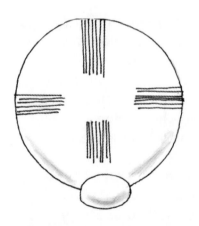

The Medicine Wheel

The Mentally Deranged

techniques to preserve their locks, you can help save them a lot of extra time and money by setting the facts straight.

Despite the endless studies and billions of dollars spent on hair loss products over the years, baldness continues to remain:

A topic that's never been fully covered.

- The fact that your grandpa on your mama's side is bald does not mean that your follicles will fossilize like his. Those designer genes can come from either side of the fence. Any way you look at it, it's hair-editary.

- Some people believe that any man with a bald patch on the top of his head is predestined to become a monk. If that is true, we now have more than 60 million latent celibates roaming the planet.

- One theory is that incessant mental activity causes your gray matter to expand in the brain, which, in turn, causes your hairs to get the shaft. If this assumption were true, all intellectuals would be bald, and all bald men would be intellectuals.

- The fate of your pate is not at all influenced by shampooing your hair once or even twice a day.

- Many people, especially wives and partners of bald men, contend that bald men are more virile. Just ask the wives, concubines, female relatives, and servants of a bald Moslem (known as a "hairem") and they'll settle the issue once and for

all. I know my wife, Janie, believes that an excess of male hormones (testosterone) prevents the production of hair. Who can argue with such intuition?

Warning! Do Not Try This At Home: To counter this presumed hormonal imbalance, the philosopher Origen tried castration. He really did! However, no record remains of the outcome. Others have actually tried ingesting female hormones (estrogen) to grow hair but discovered that either their voices raised or their breasts grew larger.

- Wearing hats and toupees does not cause hair loss, so stop blaming yourself if you've worn hats for years or played sports that required headgear.

- The hairbrush has become one of the fondest memories for millions of bald men, because they believed that one hundred strokes of the hairbrush daily would create healthier hair. You may get more luster to your cluster, but it doesn't do a thing for hair growth.

- I was told that standing on my head, hanging upside down on a back swing, or lying on a slant board for an hour each day would rush essential oxygenated blood to my head and help my hair grow back. The truth is that either your hair has a blood supply or it does not. Increased blood flow has not been scientifically shown to increase hair growth.

- Shaving your head will not cause your hair to grow back thicker. What it can do, however, is make you appear even more like a phallic symbol than you already are. Ah, the wonderful choices we have to make.

- Many individuals believe that we get our thinning hair from excess oil or sebum (secreted by the sebaceous glands) that blocks the hair follicle from growing. If this were true, persons with blocked pores would have thousands of ingrown hairs on their heads, causing hairbrained ideas to multiply like mice.

- Is there a cure for androgenetic alopecia (baldness)? Nope! Once a genuine dome improvement course appears on the scene, millions will flock to the lectern of the richest inventor on the planet.

The First Hair Growth Prescription

Take equal measures of fat from the bodies of a lion, a hippo, a crocodile, a snake, and a goat. Mix well and heat. Apply to the top of the barren scalp. —Anonymous

- And last, but surely least, is a dart board of eight other supposed causes of fallout that have been put forth at one time or another over the last 300 years. I record them here just in case you might still be holding on to one of them.

1. Since the early 1900s, guess what has been blamed for hemorrhoids, gas, insomnia, headaches, bad breath, varicose veins, obesity, and BALDNESS? Yep, none other than constipation. Thus, whatever you do, don't hold back!

2. What is it that makes you thin and makes you lean and takes the hair right off your bean? If you weeded out slimming shakes and diet pills and guessed tobacco, you're absolutely correct.

3. Laughter has been charged with first-degree denudation based on the old belief that stretching facial muscles pulls the scalp and loosens the hairs' hold. Ha! That's a joke!

4. Drinking too much beer has likewise been blamed. But I don't get it—If a thick head makes a good beer, how can a good beer make a thin head?

5. One man told me that he went bald because he had too much noogie.

   "Do you mean nookie?" I asked.

   "No, I mean noogie. It's when your big brother scrapes his knuckles over your head so much that it rubs the hair right off."

6. Since Los Angeles claims to have more bald men per capita than any other city in the world, some are headstrong in their belief that air pollution is the main source of hair diminution. Could that

explain why USC and UCLA have more split ends on their football teams than most other schools?

7. Two hundred years ago a balding man awakened one morning, and to his dismay found hair strewn across his pillow.

"How can this be?!" he asked, despairingly.

"Why it must be the headboard, George. You must be rubbing your head against the headboard," his wife surmised.

And so, for a long time afterward, balding men far and wide removed their headboards and pulled their beds away from the wall.

8. Too much sex has also been accused of contributing to the delinquency of hair. One claim is that making excessive U-turns under the sheets is the culprit, while another allegation is that sexual excitation causes too much energy to be diverted to the lower pastures. You have to feel this one out for yourself.

Thirty-Two Dynamic Ways to Have Fun with Your Head

Whether you're with friends, sports enthusiasts, children, strangers, or work associates, your head is a constant asset that can create added joy and laughter wherever you go. By practicing any of these sure-fire ways to have fun with your head, you'll soon discover how sharing your scarcity truly brings you greater abundance.

Having Fun with Your Head

> Ask not what you can do for your head
> but what your head can do for others.

Around Friends

- Tell your experience of going to the barbershop. For instance, "Last week I went to get a haircut and the barber charged me $7.00!—$4.00 to find it and $3.00 to cut it."

- When people ask you anything about your hair loss reply, "You know, hair doesn't really fall out—it grows in and comes out your ears and nose."

- Go up to a friend and say, "Give me some skin," and when he holds up his hand for the traditional high five, lean over and present your barren beacon instead.

- Show pictures of yourself when you had hair. People are always curious to see them and invariably say, "You look a lot better the way you are now" or "I just can't imagine you with hair!"

- Give your loved one a squeeze bottle of chocolate syrup as a present and invite her to play tic tac toe on your head. Be sure to inform her that she can play, but *only* if she licks the slate clean.

- When listening to a rock 'n roll song imitate a rock star by brushing imaginary hair out of your eyes with an exaggerated sweep of your hand.

- Do an imitation of a roll-on deodorant. Simply pull your shirt collar up around your ears and gyrate under a consenting friend's armpit.

- Ask someone with hair: "Who's your barber?" Once they tell you, they'll inevitably ask you with a grin, "And who's *your* barber?" "God. He always gives me a good part," you reply.

- Go up to a bald friend of yours and say, "I've got a joke that's so funny it'll make your hair fall out . . . Oh, I see you've already heard it!"

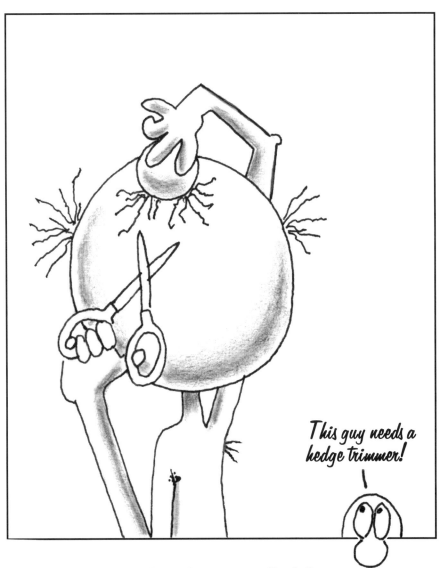

Your hair doesn't really fall out —
it grows in and comes out your nose and ears.

Using your head as a roll-on deodorant

- When you go into a barbershop always ask for an estimate. After all, it's not fair that the barber should charge you the same as someone with hair down to his shoulders.

- Tell funny stories about your head. For example, once when signing books at a promotional event, I asked an attractive African-American woman if she knew anyone who was bald. With a gleam in her eye she replied, "Not 'til tonight, honey, not 'til tonight!" What do you think she meant by that?

Another memorable event occurred when I was a member of the Jesuit Order and preparing to become a Catholic priest. I was studying Spanish and philosophy in Mexico City when I was invited to a meeting of 800 Jesuits in Veracruz, Mexico, to usher in the beginning of the new school year. While I was traveling there, unbeknownst to me, one of the Mexican Jesuits bought me a huge yellow comb from a young street vendor. The opening meeting was about to begin when the Jesuit presented me with this colossal comb. Laughter rippled through the crowd as they began noticing one by one what had just transpired. I quickly consulted my gringo friend Bill:

"Psst! . . . Bill . . . How do you say comb in Spanish?"

"*Peine* (pronounced 'pay-eh-nay')," Bill responded. I repeated it three times out loud so I wouldn't forget it.

What he didn't tell me was that the slang word in Spanish for penis was *pene* (pronounced "pay-nay") and to make sure to pronounce *peine* correctly.

At that moment, I bravely stood up to the microphone and blurted:

"Muchas gracias por mi pene grandote. Si hay alguien aqui que quisiera usar mi pene grandote, va a estar en mi cuarto." (Translated: "Thank you very much for my big penis. If there is anyone here who would like to use my big penis, it'll be in my room.")

Belly laughs broke out across the large conference hall. Many had tears rolling down their cheeks while others buckled over in hysterics. I had no idea what I had said. My friend Bill was also splitting a gut when I leaned over and received word about what prompted such a raucous response. I felt embarrassed for a few seconds and then burst out laughing right along with them. It was this experience that initiated me into this group of strangers. It was my bald head and my "pene grandote" that gave me a green card of acceptance into their community.

- Do a strip tease with your naked noggin. Cover your head with as many things as you can (e.g., scarf, wig, hat, etc.) and take a little bit off at a time while humming a seductive tune. Advanced baldies may use sensuous music, dimmed lights, and silky lingerie to add to the occasion.

Around Sports Enthusiasts

- Use your head as a bowling ball. Place thumb in mouth and middle fingers on the inside corners of your eye sockets. Put free hand on top of head and then run up and pretend (of course) to let it roll down an imaginary alley.

- Wear a headband or hat and say, "I only wear this to keep the hair out of my eyes."

- Wear a baseball cap with a ponytail coming out the back. People who know you will usually do a double-take before breaking out in laughter. And when you take off your hat around people you've never seen before, the responses are endless.

- When playing a sport like tennis or racquetball, ask your opponent(s): "I'm going to take my hat off now, do you mind?" They'll inevitably say something like, "Unfair!" or "Oh, the glare!"

Around Children

- When near a baby, gently rub the little head and say to the parent, "This kid's got more hair than I do!"

- While gazing affectionately at a little baby recite:

  Hello sweet baby with hardly a hair,
  Do you know my head is just as bare?
  Enjoy all the kisses on your soft little pate
  For until you get older, you'll just have to wait.

Using your head as a bowling ball

INSTRUCTIONS

1. With your eyes closed, place ring and middle fingers on the inside corners of your eye sockets.

2. Place thumb in your mouth.

3. Wrap your other arm around the top of your head and grasp your forehead.

4. Take 3 steps forward and pretend (of course) to roll your head down an imaginary alley.

- When visiting people with young children, invite their kids to make a wish over your head. Lean over and ask each of them one at a time to place both of their hands on your head. Then say, "Now close your eyes and wish real hard for what you want."

- Play "Name the Brain" Game. Put cling wrap securely on your head. Then have someone draw an outline (with a black easy-erase marker) of the various parts of the brain directly onto the cellophane. Then invite children to name the parts of the brain by pressing their index fingers on the specific areas or by coloring in the spaces with colored marking pens.

- Go dressed as a pumpkin head on Halloween with your curvaceous dome forming the top of the pumpkin. Buy a plastic or paper pumpkin head and cut out the bottom so that you can easily fit it over your head. Make sure there is a space large enough at the top so that just your head is showing through. Then tape the paper or real stem of the pumpkin to your head and go out with the kids and ask for treats.

- Blow up some balloons and take colored marking pens and have some children paint your face and head on the balloons. This gives the little painters a chance to really focus on your head and thus to get to know you in a fun way. Then have each child

Agnes is astonished by the accuracy of the
Gypsy's uncanny predictions using her
unusual crystal ball.

explain how his or her drawing looks like you. Give them all prizes for their wonderful creations.

Around Strangers

- Carry a comb and pull it out once in a while and say, "Would you like a comb? Up 'til now I haven't been able to part with it."

- While standing in line at a checkout counter, moan to the person in front of you, "Whew, I'm having a bad hair day!"

- Put up a bald front. Make your own T-shirts using personal photographs and quotes similar to those found in this book. For example, "Bald men are sexy," "My dad has a beautiful bald head" or "Bald men, an endangered species—protect our wildlife" are but a few of the creative possibilities.

- When you pull out your wallet to pay for something, display your membership card with a name on it such as *Skin Club for Men.* Your name, address, and "valid until death" inscription should be on the card along with anything else you want on it. For instance, you could have a catch phrase that reads, "Dedicated to winning with skin and helping others do the same."

Around Work Associates

- Wear a toupee once in a while. Since most will not recognize you at first, you will all get a good laugh once they do. You can always try a paste-on mustache or beard for added impact.

- Have pictures taken with one or more of your bald friends or relatives. Caption it with something like: "Rolling stones gather no moss" or "The Bald and the Beautiful" and display it in a prominent place at work.

- Ask some of your work associates this question: What do you get when you put two bald heads together?

    — Find another bald man with a similar skin tone to your own. Then lean over and put your heads together and have people guess what you are. Or, take a photograph of two bald heads side by side and ask people what they think it is. What do you think it is?

- When you have meetings at work that require group participation, offer to use your head as a masking tape holder. For example, when your small group is asked to write down their responses on a piece of newsprint to eventually hang on the wall for presentation, offer your head as a place to store small pieces of tape until your group is ready to present.

- Tell someone that you've found a cure for baldness that really works. When they ask "What is it?" respond:

  "Well, you put Preparation H on your head each day for a week. It doesn't grow your hair back, but it shrinks the skin to make your hair meet back in the middle."

- Buy a hardcover book with blank pages and entitle it *How to Save Your Hair.* Cut out the middle section of all the pages so that you have a square hole not seen when the cover is closed. Attach a small cellophane bag filled with hair to the back cover so that it shows through the hole when the book is opened. Lay it down in a conspicuous place with the title prominently displayed.

- During a break or at an office party, play "Can you find the bald man?" Arrange to have a group of men with hair stand near you with only you wearing a hat. Designate a person ahead of time to announce, "Okay, for a free gift, who can pick out the baldheaded man in this group?" This is a quick and easy game that can be used to spice up coffee breaks and office parties or to endear employees to a bald boss.

Bald men are the first ones to hear snowflakes.

The Bald Head: A Spiritual Symbol

Unbeknownst to most men and women, the bald head is a spiritual symbol. The quasi-round sphere bespeaks wholeness and unity, a basic yearning in us all. The vacant lot on top represents the uncluttered mind when we are able, at times, to be simply present without jumping from one thought to another. Clear, open, and unencumbered, the sky-clad dome remains grounded in the earth while touching the heavens. Thus, with the baldheaded man, mother earth conjoins with eternity and feels drawn to that ultimate Love that goes beyond any verbal description.

The ebb and flow of our sheared shoreline is but a metaphor for the reality that everything and everyone we know is gradually changing and passing away. The temporariness of hair is but a clue to life's most compelling teaching—the importance of clinging only to Love; only to that which is eternal.

The sacred space is free, radiating light in all directions. Like the sun bringing life to all that it touches, the happy bald man elicits smiles from the hearts of those who sense his joy. Like the moon warmly glowing and filling up the night sky, the bald man spreads his loving spirit by quietly conveying the truth that we are more than what we look like. We are more than how much or how little hair we happen to possess.

Like the sky spreading over the earth, the human dome symbolizes the arms of the divine enveloping us all in an embrace of universal acceptance. Smooth and unfettered with nothing to distract or divert attention, the polished peak postulates a possible world where no division or separation exists between anyone or any-thing—where humans, animals, and plants receive and exchange the universal heat of creative life and love.

Ode to Hair

Good-bye my fleeting fleece
And thank you for the stay
For keeping me warm at night
And sheltered by day.

But now that you're gone
I choose to step out,
For love, not hair,
Is the answer, no doubt.

You were always around
And a pleasure to comb,
But now that you're gone
I will flaunt my sweet dome.

I'm enjoying my head
And the world agrees
People need a good laugh
From the men of Baldese.

I now live with passion
And follow my bliss,
But you my dear locks,
I will no longer miss.

Like all living things,
I'm here for a while,
So I'm letting it go
And cracking a smile.

I've searched for acceptance
At the top of my face,
But in accepting others,
Love's filled in my place.

You helped me see the mystery
Of everything that is.
Our hair is just another clue
In life's unending quiz.

So fare thee well my homeless hairs,
I'm grateful now to know,
The secret of a happy life—
Let it go, let it go, let it go.

Receding Hare Line

**The hotter the furnace
the less snow on the roof.**

Bald Mind: Wis-dome for the Bald Soul

When all is said and done, the quality with which we have loved will stand above all heads and all things temporary as the gauge for a truly successful life.

Bald Mind invites us to:

- Understand that we did not choose to be bald, but we can choose how we think about it and how we respond to it.

- Realize that our "negative" feelings about going bald come from our negative thoughts about it.

- Change our negative thoughts about baldness and choose to perceive it in a positive light.

- See that changing ourselves is the first step to changing the world.

- Learn the art of letting go.

Our looks, hair, adornments
and admirations from others
all fade with the passing of time.

Everything we presently look to
for our source of happiness
comes and goes like the wind.

All is temporary,
constantly changing,
and will eventually pass away.

When our final curtain call arrives,
we will be impelled to let go
of absolutely everything.

Therefore, love, and learn the art
of letting go while alive.

Bald Mind invites us to:

- Let go on a daily basis of all that passes through our minds, hearts, and bodies.

- Cling only to love, to that which is eternal.

- Understand that it's not the amount of hair a man has on his head, but the amount of love in his heart that matters.

- Realize that we become whatever we put our attention on. Therefore, focus on our positive qualities and what we have to contribute to our families and the world rather than on passing things like skin and hair.

- See that hair does not make the man and that a full plume from womb to tomb is not necessary for a happy, love-full, and successful life.

- Contemplate the possibility that others will come to love us and our beautiful heads when we love them. Put positive energy and attention out and it will come back in unexpected ways.

- Understand that love is not a feeling, but something we do for another in a conscientious, gentle, and caring way. We do not get love by adding to our head cover, but by being love in a compassionate, humorous, and helping way.

- Connect with other bald men who have gotten to the other side of hair. "To know the road ahead, ask those coming back." — Chinese proverb

- Do what brings joy and significance to our life and the lives of others. Make a contribution to the world just by being ourselves in every moment.

- Realize that nothing, including hair, can *make* us happy. We can only *be* happy.

- Bring pleasure into our lives not by acquiring more hair, but by being the person who brings great pleasure into life.

- Let people know how good we are, not by how much hair we have, but by just being ourselves.

- Appreciate the difficulty we have with losing our hair and have the patience to learn its lessons.

- Free ourselves of the impossibility of trying to control what cannot be controlled. Know that all that can be controlled is the way we choose to think about hair and the loss thereof.

- Focus on our likenesses and connectedness with all people rather than on our differences. Understand that all separation (i.e., between those with hair and those without) is the opposite of union and undivided love.

- Allow what is to simply be.
  Embrace what is rather than wanting to change it.

- Wake up to the truth that most people don't really care if we are bald or not.

- Be grateful for what we have. Remember, whatever we appreciate, appreciates.

- Use our head as a gift to be enjoyed, relished, and sensually shared with the world.

- Let our hair down and enjoy the ride.

Mission Statement

Dave Beswick is committed to:

- Serving bald(ing) men.

- Supporting and working with men who are having difficulty with their hair loss.

- Educating parents, mates, and friends of bald(ing) men about what these men are going through and how to serve them in sensitive and effective ways.

- Showing men who are happily hairless how to use their heads as a positive asset in order to bring more joy and laughter into the world.

- Teaching men who have come to peace with their heads how to be mentors to younger men who are going through the often painful time of hair loss.

- Helping raise awareness that baldness is not a problem or something negative, but rather a natural and perfectly fine way to be.

Baldness is a thing of beauty.
— African (Jabo) Proverb

Life in the Hair After

 ...how bald thou art ... how **BALD** thou art.

The Value of a Smile

It costs nothing, but creates much good. It enriches those who receive it without impoverishing those who give it away. It happens in a flash but the memory of it lasts forever. No one is so rich that he can get along without it. No one is too poor to feel rich when receiving it. It creates happiness in the home, fosters goodwill in business, and is the counter sign of friends. It is rest to the weary, daylight to the discouraged, sunshine to the sad, and nature's best antidote for trouble.

Yet it cannot be bought, begged, borrowed, or stolen for it is something of no earthly good to anybody until it is given away willingly.

— **Anonymous**

Bring joy and laughter into the world

The people of the world who have the ability to laugh at themselves are those who survive.
— Jerry Lewis

A laugh can transform almost unbearable tears into something bearable, even hopeful.
— Bob Hope

Laughter is the best medicine. It can relax nerves, improve digestion, and help blood circulation.
— Dr. Norman Cousins

Laughter increases immune system activity and decreases stress-producing hormones.
— Lee Berk and Stanley Tan of
Loma Linda University Medical Center

If we were talking about a prescription that had all the physiological effects, all the psychological effects and the potential immunological effects of laughter, the FDA would be on it like crazy, regulating it and running trials on it. You wouldn't be able to get it for 10 years. What's nice about humor and laughter is that it's free, and has very few side effects.
— Ed Dunkelblau, president of
The American Association for
Therapeutic Humor

Index

Dear Reader,

Thank you for reading this book. Please write and tell us of your experiences and funny stories relating to your bald head. Include any new humorous bald quips, one-liners, and jokes. Also, if you know of any more famous bald men, please send their names along, with a short description of who they are. You may find your contributions in future editions.

We look forward to hearing from you.

Ama Publishing
P.O. Box 840117
St. Augustine, FL 32084-0117

There is more felicity on the far side of baldness than men can possibly imagine.
— Logan Pearsall Smith

SPEAKING ENGAGEMENTS

Dave Beswick does speaking engagements tailored to the needs of each group.

If you want your audiences to have fun, learn something they can practically use in their own lives, and leave inspired for living more fully and joyfully, invite Dave to speak to your group. To schedule appearances call 1-888-BALD 101 (1-888-225-3101).

TO ORDER AN AUTOGRAPHED
COPY OF THIS BOOK

Call 1-888-BALD 101 (1-888-225-3101).

TO BE PUT ON OUR MAILING LIST

To be notified of future books, tapes, and gifts for baldheaded men write:

Ama Publishing
P.O. Box 840117
St. Augustine, FL 32084-0117

Celebrate the new bald paradigm!

Cranial nudity is not a problem,
but a perfectly fine way to be.